Wounds

Fragments

Derelict

Here is what people are saying about
WOUNDS FRAGMENTS DERELICT

"Fluent in the language of hope and loss, WOUNDS FRAGMENTS DERELICT offers up pieces of a love story careening towards its familiar and inevitable end. From the delicate ruins, Carlos Gabriel Kelly has crafted a new world of hard-won wisdom, where the tender roots of romance, family and his Mexican culture intertwine. Steeped in nostalgia and shaped by the rough music of contemporary life, this is a beautiful and essential first book." — **Silvia Curbelo, award-winning poet and writer, author of "The Secret History of Water" (2015) and "Falling Landscape" (2015)**

"I love the cheer energy and passion of Carlos Kelly's voice in WOUNDS FRAGMENTS DERELICT. There is intricate range of emotion in this work the way it uplifts and brings to life various registers of language in the lyric. I love the attentiveness to detail the large, Whitmanic embrace, the insistence on living-in-the word. This is a gorgeous, memorable debut." — **Ilya Kaminsky, award-winning poet and author of "Dancing in Odessa" (2004) and "Deaf Republic: Poems" (2019)**

"In a shattering debut collection of poetry, WOUNDS FRAGMENTS DERELICT, Carlos Gabriel Kelly's first statement is a question. Much begins from the interrogative. What are love poems? Kelly answers utilizing a line break: 'Fragments not in any language.' The form borrows from the large tradition of Asian poetics, less heavily leaning on the didactic, working by juxtaposition, this poetry of implication has long been favored in United States poetics. As us Latinxs know well, it is a poetic aesthetic of much *orgullo*. Through these subtleties Kelly ensembles a formally dexterous work wound tight with pathos. This poetry has fallen through the many emotional and psychological trapdoors of love, and to open this poetry is to discover love in *La Frontera*." — **David Tomas Martinez, award-winning poet and writer, author of "Hustle" (2014) and "Post-Traumatic Hood Disorder" (2018)**

POEMS BY CARLOS GABRIEL KELLY

Introduction by Sean Frederick Forbes

FLORIDA ■ NEW YORK
www.2leafpress.org

P.O. Box 4378
Grand Central Station
New York, New York 10163-4378
editor@2leafpress.org
www.2leafpress.org

2LEAF PRESS INC. is a
nonprofit 501(c)(3) organization that promotes
multicultural literature and literacy.
Stephanie Ann Agosto, Executive Director
www.2lpinc.org

Copyright © 2019 by Carlos Gabriel Kelly

Editor: Sean Frederick Forbes
Layout and design: Gabrielle David
Poetry editor: Sean Dillon

Library of Congress Control Number: 2018951797
ISBN-13: 978-1-940939-92-6 (Paperback)
ISBN-13: 978-1-940939-93-3 (eBook)

10   9   8   7   6   5   4   3   2   1

Published in the United States of America

First Edition | First Printing

2LEAF PRESS trade distribution is handled by University of Chicago Press / Chicago Distribution Center (www.press.uchicago.edu), 773.702.7000. Titles are also available for corporate, premium, and special sales. Please direct inquiries to the UCP Sales Department, 773.702.7248.

What are love poems?
Fragments not in any language.

Para mi primo Alejandro
Para mi Familia
Para mi Gente

Contents

Medicine Woman 5

Watch Them 17

Devoured 31

Need 43

Not [Love] 55

Fragments Not in Any Language 67

Distance 81

Preface

I AM A FIRST-GENERATION Mexican-American born in San Diego, California. Both of my parents were born in Mazatlán, Sinaloa. Not long after they married, my parents moved to Tijuana, Baja California where they would raise a family. My sisters were born first, spending most of their youth growing up in Tijuana. Then, a few years after I was born, my parents decided to move the family to the U.S. so we could carve our own slice of the American Dream. The allure was due in part to the opportunities an American education could provide my sisters and I—so that we could become successful people with careers and smarts, just like my father always imagined.

My family, Mexico, and the Mexican culture, history and landscape have been and continue to play a huge role in my life; it is only within the U.S. that my identity ever became a question. I grew up Mexican, speaking Spanish *en la casa* and hearing my father continually ask me and my sisters to speak Spanish at home. Luis Miguel was the soundtrack of my early childhood; my sisters would blast his music throughout the house, singing all crazy-like. We would have family from Mexico over all the time. Our family gatherings were common occurrences; even today, we still love getting together. We always tell stories, like how my father's father fought in the Mexican Revolution, and how he carried his pistols where ever he went.

Many of my earlier family memories live inside of the first American neighborhood we called home; where I was fortunate enough to grow up around other *gente* who shared our culture and understanding for making things better for our community. That cul-de-sac was a slice of the American Dream; the majority of the neighborhood was full of first-generation parents trying to give their kids a better future. That cul-de-sac was my life and I wasn't prepared for our home being foreclosed. It was a closely hidden secret my parents withheld from me as long as they could—for my sake, but I did not understand that then.

I was fourteen during this period of transition, and by that time I was already a life-long basketball player who had an admiration for 90s rap, hip-hop, and Oasis. Losing the home became a terrible shame, and playing basketball became my outlet to subdue the pain and embarrassment. This home was the place I fell in love with reading in, devouring *Goosebumps* while lying in bed on a Saturday. Amongst my burning passion for basketball was the joy I found in literature. However, basketball would win out while reading and anything writing became the things I only ever did during school. I had to fall in love with reading again, which I did in college, but before then I found something that would fill the gap: poetry. The HBO series *Def Poetry,* hosted by Mos Def, inspired me to take up a pen and express my emotions, my thoughts, to express a version of the world seen through my eyes. Without knowing it at the time, this introduction to performing poetry would later prove one of the most powerful instances of representation I experienced.

To date, my poetic concerns remain centered on love and loss, but I aim to delve more into my culture and what it means to be a first-generation Mexican-American. This effort materializes in the way Spanish weaves throughout *Wounds Fragments Derelict,* interjecting itself amongst my English with the purpose of adding more music. Spanish is my native tongue and so I take great care in weaving its beautiful cadences into my poetry. It's not quite the same as writing or speaking in Spanglish which is more of a casual way of speaking. The line *"no se deja* quick to own Her thrown fists" in the poem "Her Medicine" is a great example of how I play with my native tongue's musicality. When I write, I allow the two languages to work together in a way that mimics the cultural fusion of my daily life.

Writing this book became an exercise in capturing the pain and vulnerability hiding behind masculinity. These poems attempt to mold, transform, and make accessible the stories of Kid-Heartbreak's loss through that exercise. I began to write through the lens of Kid-Heartbreak as a seeker and possessor of knowledge, the knowledge one gains through experience, through love and relationships, through the power of death and loss. The series of Kid-Heartbreak's knowledge poems transform into an incantation steeped in the lessons we scavenge from the ribs of things once whole. An apparition plagues the speaker through these fragments of memory, these wounds that heal, slowly, with the passage of time.

The idea for Kid-Heartbreak came to me after the majority of the collection's poems were assembled during my time in the MFA program at San Diego State University. This time proved overwhelming as I was still mourning the death of my beloved cousin, Alejandro Jiménez, and working through the end of a nearly four-year relationship. Poetry once again served as an outlet for managing the pain that was continually asking me to return. And through constant return, I became Kid-Heartbreak, a romantic gun-slinger traveling through a strange landscape toward hope amongst the vistas offered by the past. This path toward healing bound together the memories of old into a narrative; one composed of the fragments within love's rosy bubble.

These fragments are comprised of Mexican culture, love—both familial and romantic, heartbreak, nostalgia, losing the self, the memory of place, but most of all, the loss of relationships. That said, these poetic fragments follow a loosely chronological path through a relationship, where the speaker learns to navigate the pain stemming from a nostalgia tied to "Her." This character is not meant to be some romanticized ideal of what a woman should or should not be, rather, Her serves as an apparition, that through memory (or nostalgia), haunts the speaker through this collection. This particular relationship brought me closer to my language and to the family I had in Tijuana. She lived in Tijuana and so I crossed the border frequently, which also meant I got to visit more often with family. During this time, through the catalyst of a relationship, I was able to find the semblances of my culture that had been hiding in the corners of a language and a city.

Wounds Fragments Derelict is a struggle through emotions, through language, through the nostalgia that beckons us to return. The return is heavy, it is a journey, often futile like the time lost tracing letters into the wet sand on a beach, yet we return, perhaps with the goal of finding something. Hopefully, from that place that burned itself into the embers of the heart, we can grow and learn to become people who do not fear the beauty that new love can bring. Poetry is the tool I've chosen to tell the story of Kid Heartbreak. And so, this is the struggle we learn from. ∎

—Carlos Gabriel Kelly
Columbus, Ohio
September 5, 2018

Introducing Kid-Heartbreak

IMAGINE YOU FIND YOURSELF single after having been in a serious long term relationship with your girlfriend and you're unsure of how to cope with this devastating loss. It's a major shock to your ego and you're experiencing a multitude of emotions and physical and psychological aches and pains which soon turn into deep wounds. You begin to ruminate about your past life experiences and memories which flash before your eyes in jarring fragments. You feel abandoned and vulnerable and on a daily basis, you're haunted by the memories of happy and loving times spent with your ex. You're yearning to feel better, to get out of this rut but, as the cliché dictates, it *does* take time.

Now imagine that you take on an alter-ego, affectionately named Kid-Heartbreak, in which you begin to delve into what it means to be heartbroken. It's new and unchartered territory that you have to navigate through, so you turn to writing poetry as a means of retrospection and introspection to promote healing. You'll begin to learn more and more about yourself through this process, one that leads you toward storytelling and crafting poetry.

In the narrative arc presented in Carlos Gabriel Kelly's debut poetry collection *Wounds Fragments Derelict,* a reader might begin to think about poetic and song ballads. While Kelly does not explicitly employ this poetic form in his collection, one can see the ways in which he incorporates key elements of the ballad form as a means of meditative and intellectual self-expression. Ballads tell a story in which the tone is usually serious in nature and tends to deal with matters that are deeply important to an individual or a community. Most poetic ballads detail the tragic death or mysterious disappearance of a young child. Song ballads tend to focus on themes of newfound love, everlasting love, the nostalgia of a past love, and heartbreak.

One of the most popular song ballads about heartbreak is Jimmy Ruffin's "What Becomes of the Brokenhearted" released by Motown Records in the summer of 1966. It's the song that immediately comes to my mind when I think about Kelly's debut collection. In the lyrics, two lines stand out significantly: "I know I've got to find / Some kind of peace of mind," primarily because they are apropos in describing Kid-Heartbreak's quest for overcoming his insurmountable state of grief.

Kelly's ability to portray masculine vulnerability on the page is essential when it comes to understanding his use of tone, imagery, subject matter, and poetic forms employed. Kid-Heartbreak drinks from a bottle of a cheap Kentucky bourbon as he ponders his jostled emotions and soon realizes that patience is the natural remedy for what ails him. In another poem, on a trip to Tijuana, Mexico after his breakup, a profound nostalgia "opens fire" in his mind as he walks the city streets where street vendors sell *raspados*, flavored shaved ice. In this setting Kid Heartbreak remembers the trip he took to Tijuana to visit his girlfriend and how out-of-place he felt at times. It's an endearing and slightly comical memory that unsettles him but also surprisingly soothes his soul. There are short image-based poems woven throughout the collection that serve as meditative and psychic interludes that detail the intensive healing process of his mind, body, and spirit. In other poems, Kelly shapes free verse around cultural references from the popular arcade game *Street Fighter* to the romantic comedy-drama film *The Graduate* starring Dustin Hoffman. These references gain their punch in helping to highlight and expose the speaker's eclectic and quirky personality.

What's most intriguing is the way the English and Spanish languages are presented on the page—Kelly does not provide footnotes for the words and phrases in Spanish—thus the reader is immersed in the speaker's rhythmic and complex linguistic and intellectual repertoire. In doing so, each poem is executed with the intent to be read silently and then aloud in order to appreciate the rich sonic resonances of his poetic style.

Again and again, these passionate poems map the path Kid-Heartbreak takes on his journey toward spiritual, physical and intellectual wellbeing. Reading *Wounds Fragments Derelict,* it's clear to see that the poems in this collection will appeal to all readers. ∎

—Sean Frederick Forbes
Thompson, CT
August 31, 2018

Medicine Woman

Luna de Miel

your honeymoon cruise is a lie, an upgrade to a balcony suite with animal
shaped towels with chocolates on pillows, reserved, a table for two.

six nights sheathed in the bounce of waves — she flies, heels popping,
scaling that fire, that city she believes and you, motionless in Her waves

year-round-timeshare-tourist in a *Mazatlán barrio* buying up bristles
to broom the beats of Her. into a skiff you hold Her hand, shallows guide

Her right leg in when ocean pulls: *¡hay mi chancla!* you lunge like saving Her
from a movie fall, the yelp is your name; the raspy boat slivers

across Her thigh, now pink as the sandal in your smiling hand, smiling until
she peers like eyeing unpolished stone, *why would you let go?* you try to LL

Cool Her out, *but you let go,* the captain's cackle delivers you from what's next.
she tiptoes around anger, later, Her sun is *Mexicano,* a bakery of cobalts,

the sky papaya-whip *una vista* to ease forgetting, but the unforgetting
sand cloaks itself in Her pout, stares you down to the *chancla* you chose.

Her Medicine

she's five-foot-two (every inch of it too)
no se deja quick to own Her thrown fists

she rocks scrubs, dare to call Her nurse—
Doctora snap-snap (told you son) blood shoots

out Her eyes the white a vise pushin' out shine
through pupils, a funny name for knives

render a man studious. efficient, she triage
from one heart to the next, siren on

breeze at me, silent things hack wordless,
me, the knight from *Super Ghouls 'n Ghosts,*

(Arthur) hunting the night-sky, the living-in daytime.
something we had but no longer have marks the path

with a gift back to the grave of us, 3M Cardiology Littman III
Stethoscope—clings around Her neck.

Ancient Age Kentucky Bourbon: No Glass

you journey the strange—a honeymoon begs to fill your tongue
with gasoline, origins of we-myth, a shattered void

the language in you, a known thing: its music in the throat cool
learning how to speak; this is where you learn to organize

wounds fragments-derelict, where selves split in two know the shade
you can't forgive where you say future and it sounds, instead, like patience.

the dirt of syllables suspended mimic hope, this is where
otherness becomes distance, where a breath of perfume and smoke

align themselves, that is where brief tumbles into slips—*in Her room,*
my thumbs form handkerchiefs where bandages dread and context erase—

what we build is a collection of characters, yous of our i, a chatter opaque
where, in the end, mirrors survive the shadows of every unshared road.

Kid-Heartbreak's Knowledge of Medicine

i know this—
bottle-caps become ceremony become methodology
you force into a pen petitioning the reasons why you pour

i know this—
when you write a poem about love
you write about decisions

i know this—
you check the back of boxes you find words expire
find that invisibility is a synonym for healing

i know this—
Iverson said we talkin' 'bout practice? Her medicine is practice
a practice to open up a practice—so we learn, with practice

i know this—
poems are elegies prescriptions of modern medicine they say
take two lines to conjure that time honey didn't mean burden

Recover

your palms speaking
to my chest

     respira respira

you need—you leave
to the kitchen

     ocupas azúcar

fling chocolate, circle back
to my belly

Nostalgia Opens Fire in Tijuana

she didn't know chile from a candy
rubs over the bare of Her lips;
how still i pout for that *tamarindo* spice,
that inhale that bite that linger—

hot shifts the eyes the laundry-mat into a fight,
Her hot sweating this heat, arcade blaring teens
hadōken-hadōken shoryuken Ryu guru
killing *pesos* at the local laundro beat.

across the street, *fruteria* fresh *raspados*
on a Sunday just before closing, *pesos* afumble
dame dos chamangos por favor con todo. summer
statued in our simmer-down with *chaca-chacas*

cacahuates chamoy chamoy she said d*ame tu chaca-chacas*
gacho no eres; of course i gave them up because it was,
and these are the boulevards like prayers we traverse,
foolish letters to the wind—lord i don't believe in, mercy.

Bus Stop Rhythm Blues

the walk to the bus stop was ten minutes, ten minutes of inside jokes,
ten minutes holding hands, facing a sluggish return to your vacation—

iron Her labcoat Her white top Her white Dickies the night before,
this was preparation, tomorrow's breakfast spend time
to pluck a moment, add it to a countdown of lasts—

this was Her city, the corner bodega route was enough sightseeing,
each morning she'd whisper: hearts reach confidence through repetition.

research your essay for hours, *Game of Thrones* downloading behind,
episodes stacked and ready for Her study breaks, to watch Her doze off.

three months into med school she pulls two double-shifts to road trip,
earns Her one day off on my first trip planned for every three months

Tenochtitlan—

we scale up the stones of the moon; amongst our steps, we sweep
the shadows of a fading-out, we watch the sun beat ancestral

watch the ledge lure us down; tomorrow, final morning walk to the bus stop.
dreams manage the distance like bees, death is certain, so we strive to sting

only once—yet we sting. cut of Her luggage on airport tile
cut through double-doors, the proof a silhouette offers.

Museums and Their Madness

kick won't make anyone
enter the dragon
easy the sphinx
i museum kisses
bliss is it locked
i don't have
no jack no ill
will pathways go cold-trail
can one eat yahweh
or are the entrails of our song
an island a phantom limb

Watch Them

Madness is Another Word for Previous

in the tangle of our ruins, a growth-labyrinthine opens slowly
where you petition distance through the crush of teeth,
where the scramble of maps reveal that one day
the past will catch you, stranded, in the middle of living.

there is madness in you, the madness you know well.
you know the madness that comes from loving,
you know the madness you borrow from yourself,
borrow from what never was perfection — seeking refuge

in how jarred doors lead the heart into the new, astray —
how beating begins and ends in the leap of stethoscopes;
how, when it comes to Her, distance plays for keeps.

but this is surgery, you've known this from the start:
how the madness of looking back is active.

Labyrinthine

two months ago, i dreamt we were lost
like seventeen-year-old lovers in our future life,
cloaked in that cherry tomato garden.

two weeks ago, i dreamt that music festival, you swearing
i made eye contact with Paul McCartney, cut to our first slow dance,
that Melody Unchained still hungers.

last night, i dreamt about raising distance alongside need;
how, if they understood one another,
the formula against missing you would appear.

Storage Her

1.

watch them adorn space too thin for shoulders,
    these are instruments watch them long-limbed
        wave petitions to the swelter of distance, keeping it
            burden, by the gentleness of fingertips—torn.

2.

watch them point at you, snap at you,
    the person whose dreams dangle distance,
        towns become setting voices become premonitions,
            the clattering of clothes become raindrops.

3.

sounds feast on the tangle of bodies;
    watch them vivid-rude align among the drift,
        how the names for water swimming into language
            become distance become performance become weight.

4.
performance is distance is reflection is that which put away
hums the random calculations of Her name through whispers
—jangle the distance inside your bones, watch them
how nightmares of being demand formulas.

5.
watch them, the letters of Her name, lurk into the night, asking
what kind of magic drones in the spell you crave?

Kid-Heartbreak's Knowledge of Observation

i know this —
only morsels survive
the shadow of Her gaze

i know this —
the body can't be kept
inside the body can't be kept

i know this —
for every stethoscope the heart
like pollen

i know this —
Her name now
rhymes with goodbye

i know this —
at airports years traffic
in the business of leaving

Book\Marked

so we've known that stethoscopes can harm, can leave a trace
you trail behind—Her two hands clasping Her coffee, pressing,

pressing for warmth, a body bent pressing like secrets
in every coffee-clutch, the Tijuana traffic, the hospital race, the moan

of stethoscopes. she crafted you a polaroid bookmark: your first band
headlining Halloween, said she was done watching you costume

pages with the marks you love. Her hands accuse your body of too much
warmth in the bed of an August night— a new geometry.

the language of Her hands asks of you ruins,
asks of you honey— we are experts at reflection:

Homebodies

1.

you used to get upset about how big purses were
until she pulled out an open coke-can and *tortas*

at *Cinemark;* you lean your heads on each other
watching a war flick you love,

littered blasts to the head
flicker flicker everywhere...

medic!

2.

Her medicine, Her words
flak the air full of edicts

like the agreement you had:
trade dates for *Twilight* flicks.

carrilla for days, reminded you
how she crushed on Jacob-shirtless.

3.

a breeze packing fragrance

distills bract-like
to stretch its luscious
to throw the smoke you love —

in the movies,
when two leaves exchange color
call them lovers:

he a miser of Her love —
one more generous than the other.

Native to the Small of My Back, Satin Sways Against

my body, a body
to Her body, trellised —

Her tongue teaches path
with my spine —

the smoke

the smoke

the smoke

we

speak.

Understand That Loss
Does Not Understand

watching a pair of seagulls crack the air around your nose,
you're reminded of a pair of lovers no longer lovers;
around your neck, their memory, their posture bend into relic.

your body ravenous for forward, you watch them,
they watch the night.

a hungry hand, gently in your cloak,
begs the body drip into the rhythms you drink from.

watch them, bodies like mirrors,
secrets of a lover's laugh cradle their fall;
the two you watch, the body's fog.

Devoured

An Ocean Can Devour

1.

an ocean can be a museum
  it can accommodate bodies
  it can cling to remains

2.

an ocean can have an appetite
  it can devour a person's wings
  it can devour childhood promises

3.

an ocean can be an infinite thing
  it can continue its growth through ice
  it can make Pacific a synonym for death

4.

an ocean can be a magic trick
  it can convert a rock into body
  it can convert a shoe box into casket

Alejandro's Funeral in a Church in Tijuana

she sees me slunk over buried tears
on limbs of sweater, she sees me
reap sorrow beneath warmth fading
a congregation's space for an hour's rent.

because death.
the path into plots is paved
with money clips. because death.
she doesn't know what to say.

she sticks Her head out the aisle,
she sees me—quarreling eyes
in a struggle not to break.
i, a cousin to a body lost;

to the teeth of an ocean,
i cry instead of sing.
we spill our oceans,
she brings to me Her song.

Devoured When I Remember

only the mouth of

    Her fingers

        speak the language of my skin —

        open palmed

        i form

    Her hands

        the image of my slaughter.

The Milk Bandit

ma raised two brothers two sisters, one of them Her,
she remembers Her mother in the realm in the box of housework

she remembers Her brother's baby bottle in the word crave,
in the heat, a subject *Mazatlán* never had a question in—

a vestige in the shadows, a toddler squirrels, she remembers how
she knew the hour exact, Her calculations in the sounds of silence.

a wave from the *malecon* breeches time, throws a breeze through windows
in the room where she hides, lying underneath Her brother's crib

Her legs crossed with one hand wrapped behind Her head,
the other tilted to guzzle down the milk she felt was Hers.

she remembers every detail of Her thievery, remembers the taste of success,
the shouting the day she was caught, the laughter every time she remembers.

The Word Alex

what can be said

about space

how it is ~~filled~~

with a name

Devoured This Hurt Like Losing

the world we —

                                   inside

the land of the body

                                   does someone always have to own

the land
the people inside
the body
the body

                                   inside the body the land

Sour Punch Leos

Alex taught me that it was okay to doubt.
he knew it as a kid after we watched *The Prince of Egypt,*
said "i don't believe it, Moses couldn't do that shit."

two years apart, Alex was eight; dude used to eat and walk laps
around the kitchen island-counter, staring with cocoa-puffed spoon
milk drops dripping: *¿que haces?*

even my folks: *¿que haces?* this was that summer yellow
like an all out assault on the ice-cream man with a fifty.
we'd chase his song for Fudge-Pops, for BigSticks, for gum balls,

Pink Panther's eyes waiting to enter the mouth for a dollar-twenty-five,
threads upon threads of Sour Punch, laughing, eating two at a time,
Alejandro's favorite way to munch.

our birthdays six days apart—stacks of bills broken-down to child's eyes,
the most we'd ever blown. we fought a ton, the next time he visited,
i was 11 playing *Pokemon*

i punched him in the leg for cheating; next thing i know,
mi madre, well... even the homies know Alex, my cuz,
the neighborhood cul-de-sac, the whole block remember him

he'd always join the mischief. in high school, he knew about my line-work,
always said *lo quiero leer todo* and he did.
you see, he always dreamed of being a pilot,

he'd always say we'd fly together—got his license at 19
so the sky could take him from us, in the ocean waves of Oceanside,
a forever-barrier to the promise of familiar.

Mazatlán Spits Lessons

Mazatlán spits stories about when you gave up god,
the saving you never thought you'd push away
into the rattle into the urge to live without prayer

Mazatlán spits poetry from its throat through *Pacifico con limón*
o cuartitos at fourteen, drinking enough to be down to play checkers
on a board carved into a park table to play your first *peda*

Mazatlán spits street names *Calle Ángel Flores, Olas Altas,*
Aquiles Serdán; it says remember the *barrios* remember the *malecon*
the skin you used to share with Her

Mazatlán spits advice, with a wounded heart: to be reckless,
be reckless with the blue you revisit, a blue you make homes in,
be reckless with the ocean-blue midnights

Hecho Con Cariño

for Her to call between patients
to say: honey, best sandwich she ever had,
wake the thermos, sneak the strongest
sips under the machine's pruh-pruh

tripping over hands
picked ingredients, pinch the mustard,
double-up the ham steady
pepper-jack sliced *aguacate*

chips *y una coca.*
gaze, *levantate* honey— soft

in the shower, Her fingers will tendril
soap where your shoulders, injured,
no longer reach. the grind.
Sunday mornings. 4:30 *chamba.*

Outpatient

she busts out *el tigre* blanket,
a mountain of thick-warm

she throws off with kid-like
fancy to shoot me dead, a cannula

dug-in the pale veinless back of Her hand,
shooting with a wink *pew, pew-pew.*

Her love is a traveler who loves
to wander, but there's that one spot

below clavicles, above the lungs,
between arteries, velvety-blue,

veiny causeways, there—stop.

Somewhere in That Dark

reborn between lines
when the salty bite of your lip-gloss flares
neon pink, the illest shade of Her arsenal

across my face lit up in California sky;
even now, i start again my tremble.
in the silence, you are here, i am

in a transaction of the body,
hope's fallows; Her again,
the galaxy of Her—
i close my eyes.

Need

like burley men who beg for soft

in the silence of a fish tank i world

like the indecisive calm beneath

like a riverbank of sun drenched lawns

like harbors like crescendos

red-lancing waves until the naked one —

Kid-Heartbreak's Knowledge of Need

i know this—
need is light you drink, the memory of flesh cupped closely to the ear
spends eternity climbing from ankles into the knees into the rest

i know this—
when it comes to need, you feel every groove every cobble stone beat
every garden every clumsy coo curling its way to cradle Her rain

i know this—
honey is an ancient stone, an idea, a nickname that carries
a dialect learned that needs to be unlearned

i know this—
finding out about Her marriage will pull need from the past, pull you
into the void of science fiction, a reveal teaching you nothing that lets you live

There's Nothing Romantic
About a Debit Card

at the bank where i worked
i asked my co-worker how,

later on the computer application
smiling, i definitely want to look at that
every time i enter my pin. i loved it

when we were together, got stuck
with it for years after,

the card i only used for gas;
every time i filled up,
that hazy photo imprinted

under numbers, that bookmark Halloween,
that kiss, that single kiss.

Core Samples

1.

She was not
meant to be

       examined

not meant to be

       questioned.

2.

a type of drowning, though
not the lack that kills

but the rain reminding how
she garments my dark.

3.

i, a vagabond begging
for up,

light offers bread—
no gracias.

instead, the sun skitters into the abyss
of a Maytag fridge

4.

the universe precedes us
to the pillow! let's wrestle
till always voids
always.

Graduate of Need

how many times did you want to be like Dustin, asking for directions,
questions, time eating every second you were desperate to bust up

the ceremony, bust in to bust vows eloping crazy through a small town
bust back into what was. how many times did you want that magic

bus ride back to us, back to people staring at your couple-pics on a cruise ship
screaming out cuteness. how many times did you want people to call you Dustin,

be like Dustin from *The Graduate,* show your love like Dustin. won't it be something
to be like Dustin: running sloppy into that place that shines, to be like Dustin using

symbols to fight reality off. how many times, Dustin, did you wonder what's next
after you'd break-up a wedding, wonder how you only got so far as standing

on Her doorstep saying you'd fight for a dream like Dustin, bust back in
to save us from being nothing, to keep a promise, as if i were Dustin.

Not [Love]

This is Not a Love Poem

this is not a love poem nor a premonition without blood,
this is not love finding you after five years in a backyard in *Tijuas,*

this is not a breath of air back to your body, officially conjured
through calendars with their language of days and numbers

etching their way into the mind — that future never happens.
as for forgetting what you wish to forget, watch it stumble

for someone with to stay inside, stagger its rusty what-ifs.
in five years, you won't forget the sound of soft

brutal with the not-us; i, who live in the heart-
beat of Her not here; through streets, how we

used to weave together, now i scrape, a cage
to keep it all — this is, this is not.

The Worlds We Are

a   profile

a   few

snapshots

to upload

to love

you

Honey

u
   n
      r
    a
  v
    e
     l
    s

in Her voice,
possessing
— *piojito*

s
 l
into embrace,
 d
e

search for ruins of the other.

Kid-Heartbreak on the Slide

let the ritual commence: players pirouette prayers,

    plunge one   by   one   by   one. illusions wheel forward

deluge of stars' light; this light is a village

    but here there is no shine brought by priests only the dark

red of *birria los Domingos,* hangovers *con la gente de Tijuana*

    where the liminal urge the dark's damp

ignite: the gravel, the hips, the graves.

    there is no safe distance from the votive inside

collector of solitude, accuser of the world,

    tucker of pillows under hands, words left unsaid,

a name not your own a village voiced it so.

A Birthday Message

from Her in August,
that earthy darkness hears
you, drunken; let's gather—
some lovers were never here.
who guides filament-fibers to pop?
swarm the hive of paradox?
with what? a drink? a chat?
the gleam of our plates on our reflections.
who starts? enter the second man
with intelligence, dastardly, villainous,
and foul, he creeps, hidden beneath.

Evidence of How
Fragments Stay Warm

the sun — a good student, first to turn homework in and rise above the rest,
does so for four years — likes to play hide-n-seek on crooked roads

slow-bend random stretches to somehow joke with love's finesse,
she's riding passenger, bouncing Her beat-up-Chucks to our Beatles mix,

tapping on Her thighs, Her drums, while McCartney serenades the blurry
hints of olive-tint views, panoramic peek-a-boo i-slay-you. the sun peaks

through pines covered in snowy thin lace and just as i foot it down a straightaway,
the Beatles, with their solar prophecies, soundtrack the sun.

maybe it was honesty or the music or how my, "i love you" joy-filled scythed
the air to make Her cry, like Julian apple pie, genuine — warms Her.

When Night Turns to Day

the moon grooves, crosses the bottom
lip of an urgent night, grooving into me;
like Her, the groove she hums

Her red dress into the air with,
Janis-jam spreads Kozmic blues
against the universe of a stuttering room.

two planets stud fabrics of space — rings
asteroid *bienvenido al torneo,* she's first,
always storms *yo primero,*

edge into the night-carnage, impalpable
yet palpable more like delicious, Her vicious,
—an orchestra unbuttons dawn.

there is no armor for this, for honey,
for laws to loom minutes into everything.

the sweet *piojito* of this, its own groove: cool, a groove
enamored by a fortress of pillows.

An Architect's Son

for months now, a spider makes a home
in my Prius, performs magic tricks

when i sleep. in all directions,
my eight-footed Ahab casts his lines

to snag a few fluttering lights,
his trap-home glistens the warmth,

rolling over arched-dunes of my dash—morning
palm trees line roads, expose the solitude

we diagram on the air, poised
in its delivery to what we've lost.

Fragments Not in Any Language

The Ontology of Self

this is it, this is our religion; this fuse, our river-rock gray
at the hands of straw-yellow hymns, religion holds

a childhood marked full of donuts for bribes, Blockbuster games
traded for attendance to church, before it was no longer a thing,

before death wore my cousins name, suspended like
a guardian angel but with no angel to guard you,

only a bridge, gaping timber planks above the bed,
no benediction for the hazy cross of a squinting midnight.

how does the body savor what's inside the body?

with gods, with the bones you use to signal
ready — spin the self over tongues unhinged,

a pair of shoulders orphaned, muscles broken into spills,
this is the message borne out from the word:

loneliness, a religion itself, a vagabond
you beg to drop change into your basket.

After Honey

rooted in the wreck of shoe-boxes, you turn to take apart your tv,
spill back and forth between the coffee cups in your room;

through your bedroom door, dash to the medicine cabinet;
through the bathroom door to bristle your toothbrush for clues,

back on carpet toes, back through doors to the book-shelves in your room,
you flip the pages of every book, still nothing but the scent of spent words.

pursuit prioritized: every light on, posters off walls, mattress to floor,
flare the box-spring, glove the pillows, wreck a slew of clothes-hangers

don't forget to check the John Wayne coffee mug she bought you;
your band had a song with his name in the title and she loved you.

your hands this morning, too busy searching through lights beneath
the glint of doors, act like a basement . . . if there was a basement.

you watch your body shadow the body of belief, the one light
where death is bronze, where worlds once inanimate to life in seconds—

Her handwritten note in a book she bought you, the one you never read,
the one you'd never found if not for the truth we hide in boxes.

The Language of Wreckage

deep reeling into the corner of a couch,
damaged, you see visions of how bodies act
more concerned with how bodies intertwine,
you draw on recollection—

wrestle flirting bodies, pester one another
with touch, play punches, cut-in
between a movie and a street fight,
but not a street fight, just giddy fists

underneath, an onslaught of smooches,
pinches, pushing, and tugging
hair spread brown, weaving into thrown pillows.

at the kitchen table, father sits with quiet
alert until the plea *¡Señor ayudame!*
he snaps your name, victory in Her laughter.

you want to write poetry about another,
about time before or after Her, but dreams
speak in shipwreck: *here i am, forget that you're forgetting.*

Heartbreak as Marty McFly

fool around with words like i'm fourteen again,
caress with my spit, the spine of "tomorrow."

an eternal un-said spotless dappled-verse un-said,
a world un-said everything i lived un-lived

what i've lived, can i un-live your drift?
after a night huddled in your skylight dichotomized

lobotomies — lobotomize itemize my eyes strike probing
like Cyclops' vision, night learning to see through Jean's touch,

Lauryn Hillin'-me, DeLorean-me, in my space kicks back to the back-off lesson,
the first time she stubbed Her toe, my hoverboard-approach snapped

attempt to console, dare not get close, *con risa* delirious,
count it down to be sure: *¿estas bien mi amor?*

Cleaning Out Old Drawers

on days you want to strangle yourself with loneliness,
you fish for what the past saw fit to hinge behind carpentry.

in a land deforested by your estranged condition, a guiding light,
wan-light wan-one wan-bright, makes you click on Pink Floyd

to ask from a reed if this is how to Diamond, if only you had
the lungs to thrum sax, to make Her sway to your dancing breaths —

in a loop where you're the one she's mad at in the knee-bends of sleep,
you spend the pitch of a solo undressing hurt of Her flipping-curls.

a series of octaves floats you between books to a sealed envelope
hiding for years, an entire house, the language she said
she would teach you if you ever asked.

Names are Boulders

there is a voyage you brave, braving the river-sirens of a name
you dare not drink, a delirious remedy to the delirium.

a barista shouts a name, Her name veers in the air
strikes the wind out your chest, flings you onto a stool,

sitting because, in this hipster-crowded coffee-shop, names are boulders.
they teach you to sip on buckets full of letters like hooks,

their cut like the milk of steel in the fibers of citrus-filaments, making homes
between teeth; we loosen them through tongues sucking on the air we lose —

here travels back to where here was then, there where time rotates
a rolodex of images like the meat-spitted spit before savoring; i seek Her

name, patient, slowly, bending down, prone to peek beneath cars
just in time to watch the smog chase away the syllables of Her name,

flittering at the party we met at, *yo who is that?* Her name
unfurls through Spanish, inside, the body groans like hinges.

i isn't me anymore, just a letter in a name in a time that flattens
for 25 cents, a tourist penny-birthmark on Her left thigh, my fingers trace,

still in the mind writing poems about the day we met, the day she left.
this coffee-shop call marks the finale of the magic you spend

summoning decay; ask it to save you from not asking why —
language bridles you, ties your tongue around a name.

Kid-Heartbreak Mishears
Her Name in a Coffee Shop

i know this—
Her language is an island, a lifejacket, a sea vessel
tongue you were fluent in

i know this—
reverberations petition you to speak fragments you leave unspoken,
fragments of healing within the crawl and beg of language

i know this—
en español o inglés you slide through los trucos de idioma,
tonight you visit, tomorrow you drown

Not the One

this is my Mordor: a laundry detergent cap full of burning change,
loose, mixed among it, a ring, the one i swore an oath to like Frodo;

engraved on the inner lining, the towers of a currency forgotten — *amor y fe
tu y yo por siempre* — forged in the consequence of a promise

the ring carries, attached to its gleam, our language in plucking whispers,
tempting me to sink into its slip once more to make invisible the past,

to make sure that the next time i promise, i understand
the gravity of pennies, understand how rust is another word for change.

Distance

How Legend Holds

immigration, dual-citizen, seven-times moved-in feeling, the desert between
        —*dos idiomas* never prepared you for the benediction of heartbreak,

never prepared you for learning to swallow like medicine
        —without water, a name you still can't—

still whispers, labor-on wrapped
        —in the noose of rumors spoken suddenly,

small things begin their bloom, still inside
        —the drunken scrawlings of hope in theories you labor.

carvings remain, trimmed out from snippets of legend, but a legend
        —nor a name does not name itself—branch through shadows,

a tongue plays where a tooth used to be
        —nestled within the comfort of gums;

this is the way stories hold on, how they survive your laboring
        —through pages to understand the meaning of *alivio*.

Espíritu Santo at the Border

on the border, you find origins split you pledge allegiance,
you find distance in candied violet; in the void, you find Her

passenger seat clings to minutes-turgid disguised as Her medicine;
with the Sentri-Pass, you scatter back across quickly, you wait,

you find Her on the corner by the meet-up-spot the Jack in the Box,
wait for Her to cross, to bridge the distance through documents.

on this journey, you reacquaint yourself with the boy rehearsing father;
with your eyes, you signal what's to be said, you practice what to say,

práctica lo que vas a decir, you turn index and thumb into a crossing
cross across my forehead before you whisper the go-to-script for crossing.

a front to your crossing, the rehearsal fades into the two cars in front: Sentri,
ready to declare nothing as you cross; *cruzar lineas,* to declare U.S. citizen.

why are bodies made to rehearse what you'll always be?

after, one day you'll cross, accidentally drive back to the Jack to pick Her up,
but you forgot how distance is another word for border, how bodies always carry it.

Honey the Dog

i'm stuck in my baby walker with Honey's paws balancing intentions
on the edge of the walker with one lick each, we shared my lollipop,

en Tijuana, where we lived before crossing into the American dream,
my mother remembers a lollipop—while hanging clothes on a line,

mother shrieked *¡Carlitos, que haces!* shrugging, she went back to her clothes,
as the third child, she must have been at ease thinking *nimodo* with the joy

Honey and i shared, a peace we'd always share.

for 16 years, she was family; ten of those, the sum of my time.
at family gatherings, we retell the stories we all hold, keep the same trajectory
after the infamous lollipop, we cross back to Tijuana, pregnant with me

my mother is sick and Honey, for two days, hadn't been seen. up and down
the neighborhood, search parties of *tías y tíos, primos y primas,* my sisters.

cuddled underneath my mother's bed, father found Honey, a guardian
on her watch, a best friend who felt the offs in mother's vibes. the day she died,

we huddled in tears in the living room; on my mother's lap, we mourned what
we knew was coming—vividly, we remember how Honey survives the distance.

Kid-Heartbreak's Knowledge of Distance

i know this—
choking inside the shadow of a votive's prayer,
an examination, designed to manufacture longing

i know this—
distance is a promenade of lips taunting, holding, planting you
into the clap of cruise-ship parquet floors

i know this—
in every forgotten limb clings how she used to touch your arm;
in every breath for forward in every shatter, reflection

Carrilla is Time Travel

carrilla time travels you back through drives to *La Presa en Tijuana*
to pick Her up for dates where distance saw itself a barrier to you
thinking you two would work,

how borders, once untenable, became your daily crossing
into the lessons of *carrilla;* Her brothers taught you through grillin',
but distance was a youngling then, you didn't fear its claws just yet.

carrilla made you the one upset after every joke until you were told
tranquilízate—but when you're considered the *gringo,*
Spanish rolls itself harshly off the tongue, bruising

distance to a language in you broken, not knowing
that *el que se enoja pierde,* Her go-to when in you,
she'd see that anger set its sails.

tranquilízate is a warning teaching you how to take a joke
that *carrilla* can cut close, can travel you back
to how *tranquilízate* is just another lesson we fail.

Beatrix Kiddo Cuts Distance

1.
Beatrix Kiddo is the kind of name you don't forget, she 's the type
to chat with her big toe, says wiggle wiggle, but it ain't a dance-off;
she's got plans to cut the distance down, to cut up the floors later

2.
Beatrix Kiddo suffers Pai Mei's wrath to add to her arsenal
the one-inch punch, a bloody fist she chops up a coffin with,
chops up the distance to her daughter, to who she's after next

3.
Beatrix Kiddo plucks an eye from you, makes you see
out of rage stuck inside the distance it takes a snake
to Black Mamba its way to your flailing

4.
Beatrix Kiddo slays names, takes names, puttin' in work all day
to Kill Bill; and yet, you're most like Hanzo: used to being in silence,
writing a name on dusty glass about the distance we find inside.

Run like Forrest

you find distance in unheard of places, in *pesos,* in *Pulparindos,*
in cable reruns of *Forrest Gump.* you find in the distance how

Forrest runs from rocks roped by bullies, listens fully to Jenny's command,
you always wonder what pushed him off that rocking-chair to cross country

run across seasons, to see the sun dig its reflection into bodies of water.
—Forrest's shadow creeps into the shot to the drop of "Running on Empty,"

it reminds you how empty handed you run, how running isn't for sport,
how you run from distance; like Forrest you "thought about Her a lot."

every time, what gets you, trudging through the Washington Monument,
Jenny shouting Forrest, or how off the stage Forrest runs into her arms,

this is the power of distance: it puts names in your mouth ready to shout
until, like Forrest, you're ready to bury the names that left their mark.

The Orange Tree at 547 Port Harwick: Her Favorite Anecdote

four-years-old in the home of my youth playing near the orange tree,
three-years-old going strong, bearing just a few orbs of fruit.

in the shuttering dance between hands and mower, father saw to the lawn;
i see him, to the brim with ice cubes a cold glass of coke in hand, *descanso*.

on one of his turns to click the mower back across, eyes fall upon the tree
missing every thing but a single leaf, the mower clacks to a still

father tilts his head, investigates, moves closer, proceeds to dust his feet,
mat welcomes his weight distributing what would be a bellowing inquiry:

¿Quien corto las naranjas del árbol?

four-years-old, but the gravity attached to his question needed no explanation,
shook my head without a peep, but pops already knew, changed his approach:

¿Quien corto las naranjas del árbol?

voiced in baby-coo sweetness—my parents' laughter at the retelling,
fond of the distance crossed to then—his question was enough to stir

my innocence, four-years-old with pride, shaking my head yes: *yo fui papá*

Acknowledgments & Extra Love

Gracias a mi familia por apoyarme, por ser la fundacíon de mi ser, los amo, siempre están en mi corazón.

Thank you to Frederick Luis Aldama, you're guidance and support led to this manuscript making it out into the world, and I'll forever be grateful. *Gracias Profe.*

Thank you to Sean Frederick Forbes for taking a chance on me and my book. I am truly fortunate to have been able to work with you so closely; thank you for your kindness.

Thank you to Gabrielle David for all your efforts in making this collection come together. Your patience and wizardry for creating books is highly appreciated.

Thank you to Ilya Kaminsky, your passion is undeniable, contagious, and exactly what MFA students need. You inspire me with your teaching, with your questions, I have truly learned a great deal from you.

Thank you to Sandra Alcosser for your kind words, guidance, and heart; you are an amazing human being. Thank you for caring so much about your students.

Thank you to William Nericcio for being there for me, (especially where there are not many of us *gente*) and inspiring me to be the best professor/ writer/student/person possible. Thanks for busting my ass.

Thank you to Kevin Dublin & Hari Alluri for supporting the dream with love and feedback. Y'all helped make this possible.

Thank you to friends who listened to poetry after long nights of music, homework, and merriment. I love you, Adrian, Anthony, Benny, Carina, Chris. <3 Comet Calendar

Thank you to the Guild: Bryan, Ivan, Jorge, Justin, and Pablo. Homies for life.

Thank you to my poetry family at SDSU, our time together will always be cherished.

Thank you to those of you who are kind enough to have bought or borrowed or stolen this book, I truly appreciate your time with my words.

Thank you to *Barzakh Magazine* for publishing "Names are Boulders."

Thank you to *Pacific Review* where "The Worlds We Are" appeared as "Going Online."

Thank you to San Diego Poetry Annual for publishing the song "She's Been Accepted to Med School in Mexico City," which partly appears here as "Bus Stop Rhythm Blues." ∎

About the Poet

CARLOS GABRIEL KELLY is a first-generation Mexican-American and second-year Ph.D. student at the Ohio State University in the Department of English specializing in Latinx Literature in the U.S. with an emphasis on poetry and video games. His work has appeared in *PacificREVIEW: A West Coast Arts Review Annual, Poetry International,* and *Studies in 20th & 21st Century Literature.* Kelly has an MFA in Poetry, an MA in American Literature, and a BA in English from San Diego State University. WOUNDS FRAGMENTS DERELICT is Kelly's debut poetry collection. ■

Other Books by 2Leaf Press

2Leaf Press challenges the status quo by publishing alternative fiction, non-fiction, poetry and bilingual works by activists, academics, poets and authors dedicated to diversity and social justice with scholarship that is accessible to the general public. 2Leaf Press produces high quality and beautifully produced hardcover, paperback and ebook formats through our series: 2LP Explorations in Diversity, 2LP University Books, 2LP Classics, 2LP Translations, Nuyorican World Series, and 2LP Current Affairs, Culture & Politics. Below is a selection of 2Leaf Press' published titles.

2LP EXPLORATIONS IN DIVERSITY

Substance of Fire: Gender and Race in the College Classroom
by Claire Millikin
Foreword by R. Joseph Rodríguez, Afterword by Richard Delgado
Contributors Riley Blanks, Blake Calhoun, Rox Trujillo

Black Lives Have Always Mattered
A Collection of Essays, Poems, and Personal Narratives
Edited by Abiodun Oyewole

The Beiging of America:
Personal Narratives about Being Mixed Race in the 21st Century
Edited by Cathy J. Schlund-Vials, Sean Frederick Forbes, Tara Betts
Afterword by Heidi Durrow

What Does it Mean to be White in America?
Breaking the White Code of Silence, A Collection of Personal Narratives
Edited by Gabrielle David and Sean Frederick Forbes
Introduction by Debby Irving, Afterword by Tara Betts

2LP UNIVERSITY BOOKS
Designs of Blackness, Mappings in the Literature and Culture of African Americans
by A. Robert Lee
20TH ANNIVERSARY EXPANDED EDITION

2LP CLASSICS
Adventures in Black and White
by Philippa Schuyler
Edited and with a critical introduction by Tara Betts

Monsters: Mary Shelley's Frankenstein and Mathilda
by Mary Shelley, edited by Claire Millikin Raymond

2LP TRANSLATIONS
Birds on the Kiswar Tree
by Odi Gonzales, translated by Lynn Levin
Bilingual: English/Spanish

Incessant Beauty, A Bilingual Anthology
by Ana Rossetti, edited and translated by Carmela Ferradáns
Bilingual: English/Spanish

NUYORICAN WORLD SERIES
Entre el sol y la nieve: escritos de fin de siglo / Between the Sun and Snow: Writing at the End of the Century
by Myna Nieves, translated by Christopher Hirschmann Brandt
Bilingual: English/Spanish

Our Nuyorican Thing, The Birth of a Self-Made Identity
by Samuel Carrion Diaz, Introduction by Urayoán Noel

Hey Yo! Yo Soy!, 40 Years of Nuyorican Street Poetry, The Collected Works of Jesús Papoleto Meléndez
Bilingual: English/Spanish

LITERARY NONFICTION
No Vacancy; Homeless Women in Paradise
by Michael Reid

The Beauty of Being, A Collection of Fables, Short Stories & Essays
by Abiodun Oyewole

WHEREABOUTS: Stepping Out of Place, An Outside in Literary & Travel Magazine Anthology
Edited by Brandi Dawn Henderson

ESSAYS
The Emergence of Ecosocialism, Collected Essays by Joel Kovel
Edited by Quincy Saul

PLAYS
Rivers of Women, The Play
by Shirley Bradley LeFlore, photographs by Michael J. Bracey

AUTOBIOGRAPHIES/MEMOIRS/BIOGRAPHIES
An Unintentional Accomplice: A Personal Perspective on White Responsibility
by Carolyn L. Baker

Trailblazers, Black Women Who Helped Make America Great
American Firsts/American Icons, Vols.1 and 2
by Gabrielle David, Introduction by Chandra D. L. Waring, Edited by Carolina Fung Feng

Mother of Orphans
The True and Curious Story of Irish Alice, A Colored Man's Widow
by Dedria Humphries Barker
Introduction by Cathy J. Schlund-Vials

Strength of Soul
by Naomi Raquel Enright

Dream of the Water Children:
Memory and Mourning in the Black Pacific
by Fredrick D. Kakinami Cloyd
Foreword by Velina Hasu Houston, Introduction by Gerald Horne
Edited by Karen Chau

The Fourth Moment: Journeys from the Known to the Unknown, A Memoir
by Carole J. Garrison, Introduction by Sarah Willis

POETRY
Ransom Street, Poems by Claire Millikin
Introduction by Kathleen Ellis

Wounds Fragments Derelict, Poems by Carlos Gabriel Kelly
Introduction by Sean Frederick Forbes

PAPOLíTICO, Poems of a Political Persuasion
by Jesús Papoleto Meléndez
with an Introduction by Joel Kovel and DeeDee Halleck

Critics of Mystery Marvel, Collected Poems
by Youssef Alaoui, Introduction by Laila Halaby

shrimp
by jason vasser-elong, Introduction by Michael Castro

The Revlon Slough, New and Selected Poems
by Ray DiZazzo, Introduction by Claire Millikin

A Country Without Borders: Poems and Stories of Kashmir
by Lalita Pandit Hogan, Introduction by Frederick Luis Aldama

2Leaf Press Inc. is a nonprofit organization that publishes and promotes multicultural literature.

FLORIDA ■ NEW YORK
www.2leafpress.org